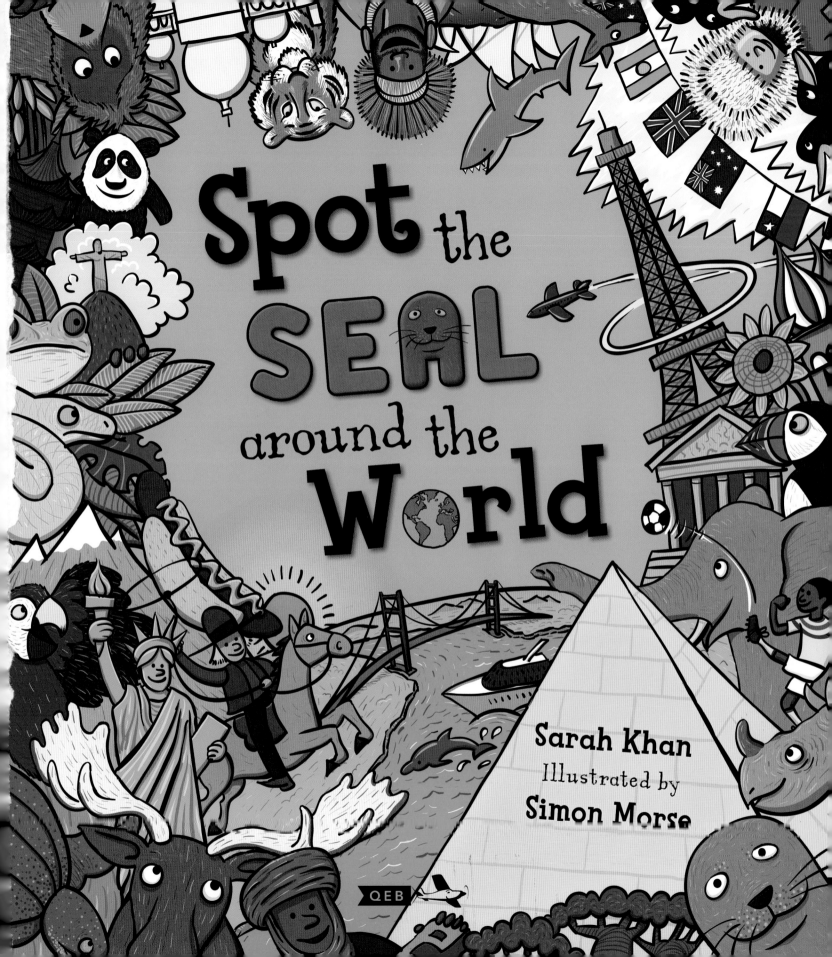

Spot the SEAL around the World

Sarah Khan

Illustrated by
Simon Morse

QEB

WELCOME TO THE WORLD!

There's lots to see. Come and have a look!

North America

Hats of the world

Flags of the world

South America

Europe

Asia

Africa

Oceania

Antarctica

Key for maps
- Ice
- Tundra (frozen ground)
- Land
- Forest
- Desert
- Mountains
- Land not part of continent

N
W E
S

This seal is hiding inside the book. Can you find him in every scene?

Caribbean Islands

Dominican Republic

Trinidad and Tobago

Puerto Rico

Haiti

Jamaica

Cuba

Belize

Honduras

Nicaragua

Panama

Costa Rica

Guatemala

El Salvador

Mexico

PACIFIC OCEAN

Can you spot these things?

moose

ox and cart

Golden Gate Bridge

cactus

piñata

beaver

North America is the only continent that has every type of climate, from the frozen ice fields of the far north to the hot rain forests of the south.

South America

Over a third of South America is covered by rain forest, which is home to millions of different types of plants and animals.

French Guiana

Guyana

Suriname

Brazil

Venezuela

Colombia

Ecuador

Peru

Bolivia

Can you spot these things?

necklace   feather   star   tassel   red flower

Lots of countries and cultures have traditional clothes. These are sometimes worn every day or just for special occasions.

Which hat do you like the best?

Europe

Europe is made up of more than 50 countries. It contains both the biggest country in the world, Russia, and the smallest one, Vatican City State.

Iceland

United Kingdom

NORTH ATLANTIC OCEAN

Ireland

Netherland

Belgium

Luxembourg

France

Switzerland

Can you spot these things?

daffodil   lynx   waffle

racing car   salamander

Portugal

Spain

Andorra

Monaco

Africa

NORTH ATLANTIC OCEAN

Morocco

Tunisia

Libya

Algeria

Western Sahara

Mauritania

Mali

Niger

Chad

Cape Verde

Senegal

The Gambia

Guinea-Bissau

Guinea

Sierra Leone

Liberia

Burkina Faso

Nigeria

The Ivory Coast

Ghana

Togo

Benin

Cameroon

Central African Republic

Equatorial Guinea

Gabon

Congo

Angola

Namibia

SOUTH ATLANTIC OCEAN

Can you spot these things?

drum

elephant

penguin

gerbil

pyramids

waterfall

Asia

Russia

Kazakhstan

Georgia
Azerbaijan
Turkey
Armenia
Lebanon
Israel
Syria
Jordan
Iraq
Kuwait
Bahrain
Qatar
Saudi Arabia
Yemen
Oman

Uzbekistan
Turkmenistan
Iran
United Arab
Emirates

Kyrgyzstan
Tajikistan
Afghanistan
China
Pakistan
Nepal
India

Maldives

Sri
Lanka

Can you spot these things?

Marco Polo sheep	tarsier
orangutan	coffee
camel	scorpion

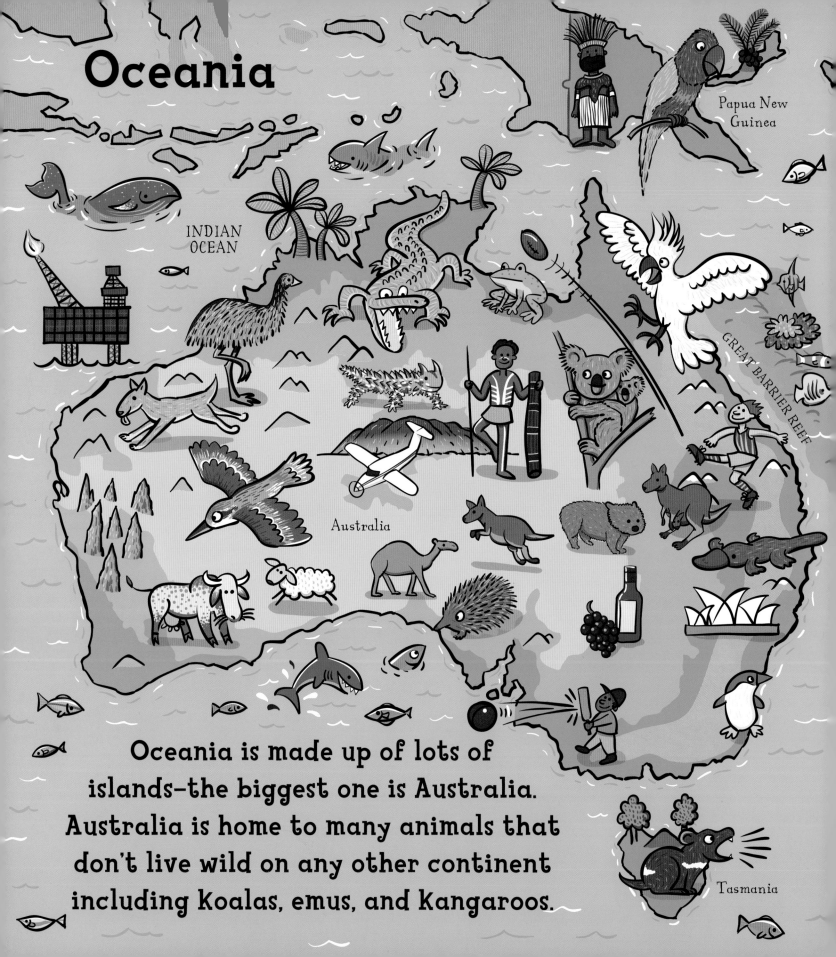

Oceania

Papua New Guinea

INDIAN OCEAN

Australia

GREAT BARRIER REEF

Tasmania

Oceania is made up of lots of
islands-the biggest one is Australia.
Australia is home to many animals that
don't live wild on any other continent
including koalas, emus, and kangaroos.

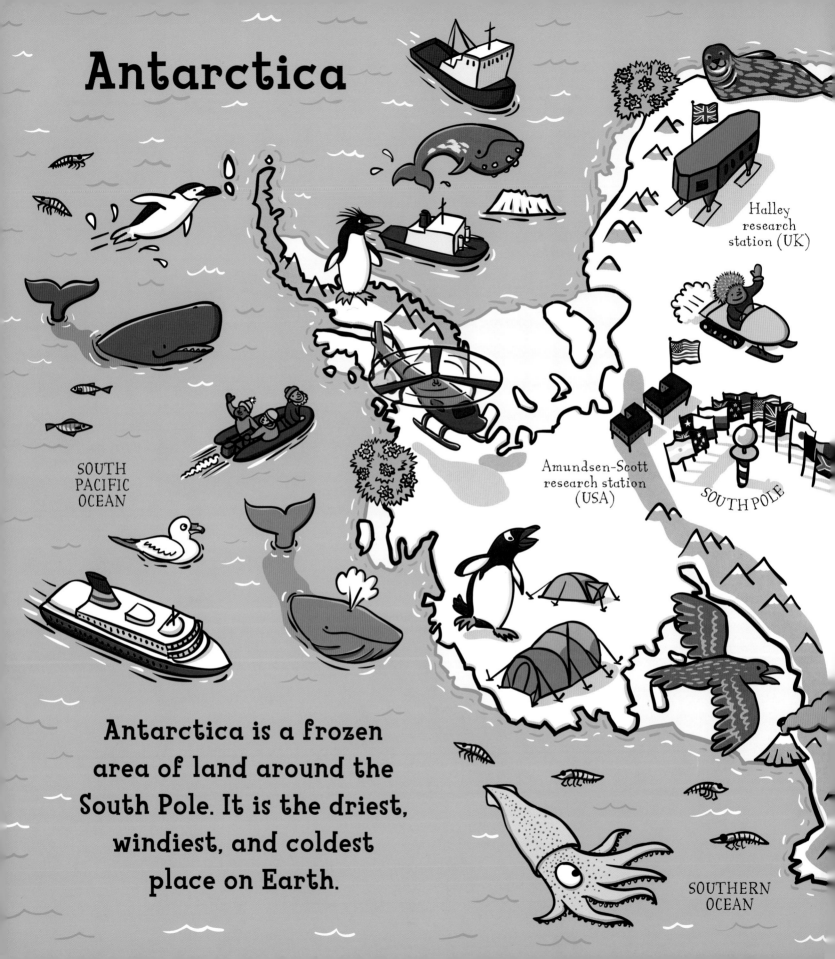

Antarctica

Halley research station (UK)

Amundsen-Scott research station (USA)

SOUTH POLE

SOUTH PACIFIC OCEAN

Antarctica is a frozen area of land around the South Pole. It is the driest, windiest, and coldest place on Earth.

SOUTHERN OCEAN

Every country has its own flag. The colors and symbols on a country's flag represent different things about that country.

Do you know your country's flag?

More to spot

Find out where these people come from by matching the numbers to the countries.

Did you find me?

Chichen Itza was a city built by the Maya people more than 1,000 years ago. Can you find a temple on the map of Mexico?

Black forest cake comes from Germany. Can you find the cake on the map of Europe?

Taj Mahal means "Crown Palace." Can you find the palace on the map of India?

The carnival in Rio de Janeiro is the biggest in the world. Can you find the dancers on the map of Brazil?

1. Nigeria
2. Netherlands
3. Mexico
4. France
5. United States of America
6. India
7. Russia
8. Thailand
9. China
10. Japan
11. Colombia
12. Poland
13. Finland
14. Mongolia
15. Angola
16. Afghanistan
17. Jamaica
18. Pakistan
19. Argentina
20. Iran
21. Saudi Arabia
22. South Africa
23. Algeria
24. Germany
25. Morocco
26. Brazil
27. Peru
28. United Kingdom
29. Hungary
30. Australia

Flags of the world

Greece	Russia	France	Sweden	United Kingdom	Italy	Switzerland
Poland	Spain	Germany	Norway	Mexico	Canada	United States of America
Jamaica	Brazil	Argentina	Chile	Ecuador	China	Japan
Malaysia	Thailand	Sri Lanka	Jordan	Vietnam	India	Pakistan
Morocco	Ghana	South Africa	Kenya	Nigeria	Australia	Tonga

The most popular colors on national flags are red, white, and blue.

More than a billion flags are made each year.

These flags are all from different countries. Can you find the countries in the book?

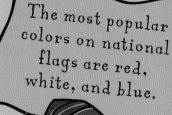

More world fun!

National flag

Paint or draw the design of your country's flag on a rectangular piece of paper—or make up your own design! Wrap the left edge of the paper around a pencil. Secure it with tape, then wave your flag.

Italian pizza

Spread ketchup or tomato puree over pita bread or a bagel. Sprinkle some dried or fresh herbs on it. Add grated cheese and any other toppings you like. Ask an adult to cook your pizza in the oven for 10 minutes.

Hide and seek

Choose a cuddly toy that you can hide around your home for a friend or family member to spot, just like the seal in this book! You could hide other objects too and make a list of things to find.

Memory game

All you need for this game is some friends! The first player says, "I went on holiday to . . ." and names a country. The next player repeats the sentence and adds another country, and so on. You can use this book to help you think of countries. The game continues until someone can't remember the list or makes a mistake.

Publisher: Zeta Jones
Associate Publisher: Maxime Boucknooghe
Editorial Director: Victoria Garrard
Art Director: Laura Roberts-Jensen
Editors: Tasha Percy and Sophie Hallam
Design: Duck Egg Blue and Mike Henson

Copyright © QEB Publishing, Inc. 2016

First published in the United States by
QEB Publishing, Inc.
6 Orchard
Lake Forest, CA 92630

www.qed-publishing.co.uk

A CIP record for this book is available from the Library of Congress.

ISBN 978 1 60992 823 0

Printed in China